Dedicated to anyone who has/had vaccine injuries and reactions.

We will continue to spread the awareness — you are a warrior!

Parents — it is not your fault.

The sun seeped in through the bedroom window as Wesley did his morning stretch. He looked down the bed to see his little toes sticking out from the blankets. He gave them a wiggle and started to giggle.

Wesley turned toward his teddy bear and said, "Wake up, Pookey. Today I go see the doctor for my shots. I'm scared. I don't like needles, they hurt. I need you to come with me."

The door creeped open and Wesley heard his Mom. "Good morning my dear boy, and you too Pookey." She gave them both a loving poke as she giggled.

Wesley swung his feet around, landed on the floor and scratched his head.

"Mama, what time is my appointment?" he nervously asked.

His mom replied, "In about an hour, which means we must get you dressed and have breakfast." She watched Wesley twirl his curly blond hair with his finger.

"Being six years old is tough. I just want to go outside and ride my bike or go to the park with you." Wesley explained.

"You know, Wesley, there is nothing to be afraid of. Yes, getting your vaccinations hurts a bit, but it's for your own protection and for everyone else around you. You don't want to get sick, do you?"

"No, Mama, I don't. I just have a bad feeling about this."

Wesley's mom was digging through his drawers, trying to find matching socks. "Ah-ha! Found a matching pair!" she exclaimed with satisfaction. "Here, put on your socks, sweetie, and stop worrying." She smiled and handed him the socks. "Everything will be fine. You've been through this before."

Wesley reached for the socks, but he wasn't convinced.

Down the stairs he went hand in hand with Pookey. Wesley's mom called him into the kitchen for some scrambled eggs and avocado. After breakfast they walked to the front door to get their shoes and jackets on then they left the house and got into the car and went on their way.

Once they were at the doctor's office, the nurse took Wesley and his mom into a little room. She weighed Wesley and made him stand up tall so she could measure his height. Then she smiled and said, "Doctor Sam will be right in," as she turned to leave the room, shutting the door behind her.

Wesley, still feeling nervous, jumped up on the examination table and his mom sat down in a chair beside the table. Wesley looked around him. He noticed the doctor's tools on a tray as he started to feel nervous again.

"Knock, knock," the doctor said as he walked into the room. "Hi there, Wesley." He nodded a greeting to Wesley's mom. "How is everyone doing today?"

"We're doing well," replied Wesley's mom for the both of them.

The nurse walked in with a tray for the doctor.

"Okay, Wesley, we are going to give you two needles today."

"It will sting a bit, but then you will be good as new. When we're done, Nurse Betty will give you a sticker and a lollypop. But you have to be a good boy and sit still for me." Doctor Sam looked at Wesley's mom and nodded his head. "Let's proceed."

Wesley held onto Pookey tightly."Okay, Nurse Betty, please hand me the first needle." Nurse Betty handed the needle to the doctor and wiped a clean place on Wesley's arm.

Wesley looked at his mom and gripped her hand. "I'm scared, Mommy. I don't want it to hurt."

Wesley's mom squeezed his hand gently and assured him everything would be okay. "It's okay, son. You're such a brave boy. When we're done here, I'll take you out for ice cream."

After the second needle, Wesley's eyes were watery from the tears he was trying not to cry. It had hurt and burned a lot.

"You did great, Wesley!" Doctor Sam exclaimed. Follow Nurse Betty out for your sticker and lollypop."

Wesley wiped away his tears, hopped down off the exam table and hugged his mom. "I never want to do this again, okay?"

"I know it hurt, sweetie, but now you won't ever get sick with the chicken pox or measles. It's for your own good. You're also protecting those who can't be vaccinated." She hugged Wesley tightly.

Later that afternoon, Wesley lay on the couch. He was too tired to play. His mom walked into the living room and asked if everything was okay. "I'm not feeling well. Both my legs hurt and burn."

Wesley's mom pulled up the blanket and gasped. "Oh my goodness! Your legs are swollen and very red." She tried not to let him see her panic. "I'm going to call Doctor Sam right away."

She took her cellphone into the kitchen so Wesley couldn't hear and called the doctor's office. Wesley's mom explained to Nurse Betty what had happened, and Nurse Betty told her it was a normal.

"How is it normal?" Mom asked.

Nurse Betty said it was a common reaction to the vaccines and that it was nothing to worry about.

Wesley's mom hung up and decided to take Wesley to a different doctor right away.

She got him into the car and started crying. "I am so sorry, baby. I didn't know this could happen." She said, wiping her tears as she buckled herself in.

"We all make mistakes. I knew it wasn't a good idea. I could feel it in my heart." Wesley tried to comfort her with his words.

"The doctor I'm bringing you to now is a naturopathic doctor. She uses natural medicine. Let's see if she can help," she said and started the car.

Wesley smiled and put his head back on the booster seat. "As long as there are no more needles, I'm okay with that," he said with a sad look on his face.

They entered the doctor's office and were greeted by the receptionist. She took them to the exam room and checked his weight and height. The doctor walked in. "Hey, you must be Wesley. I am Doctor Sandra. I heard you had a possible reaction to the vaccinations. May I check your legs and your temperature?"

Wesley lay back on the examination table. "Yes, you may."

Doctor Sandra tugged up the bottom of his shorts and had a look. "Yes, it feels very hot on the red area." she said as she turned to Wesley's mom. "Okay, Wesley, now I'll check your temperature." She put the thermometer in his mouth and, when it beeped, she took it out to have a look. "Your temperature is 101 Fahrenheit. You have a fever because your immune system is fighting off the toxins that were injected."

"Toxins?" Wesley's mom asked.

"Oh, yes," the doctor said to her quietly while Wesley fiddled with the stethoscope, "Some vaccines have different types of DNA and many toxic ingredients that we should never consume in any way. The doctor turned to Wesley and explained in a louder voice, "Our bodies work hard to fight against the things that aren't good for it and that's why you got a fever. Your body is trying to burn out the bad stuff. You are having a vaccine reaction, Wesley."

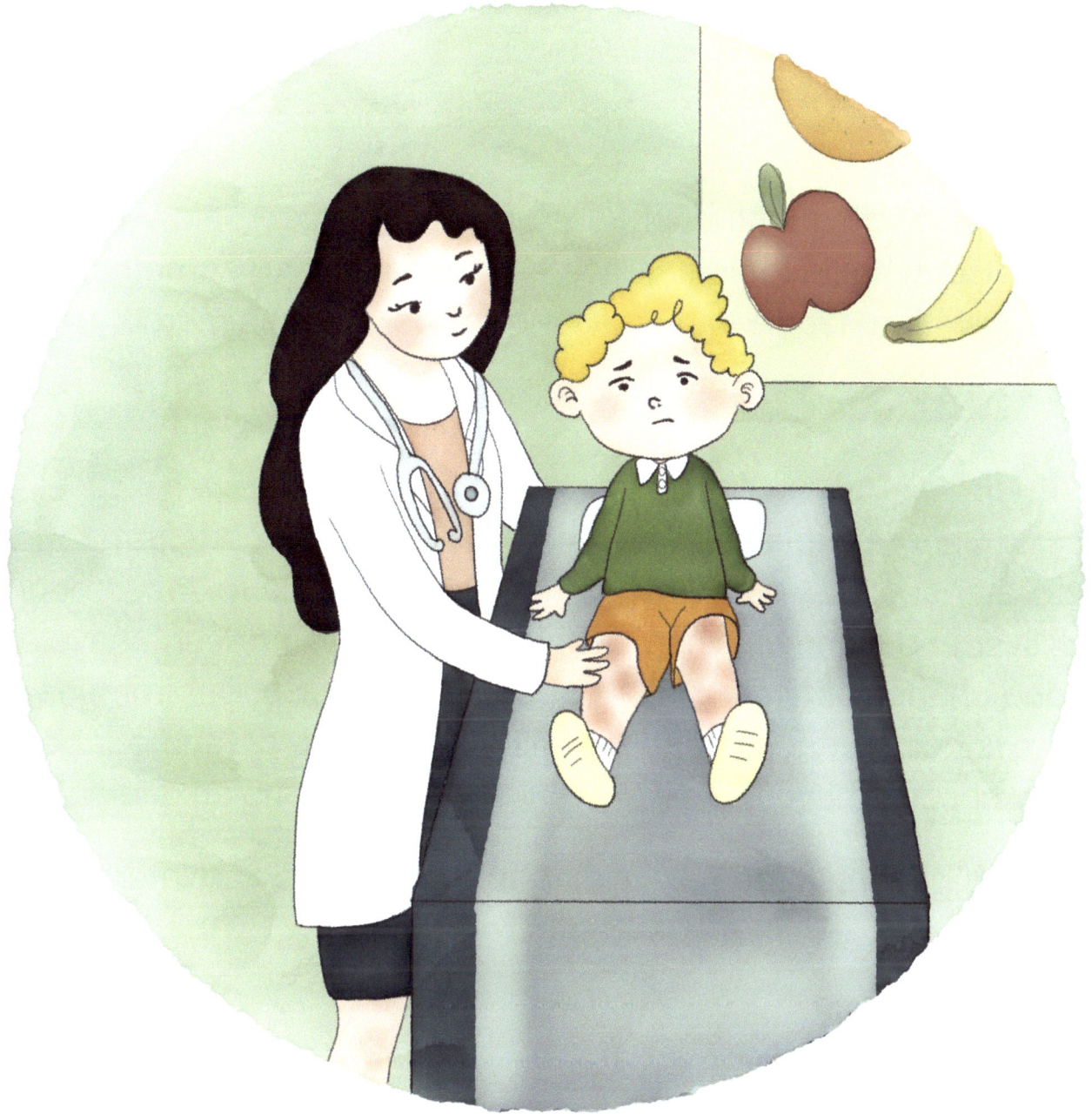

"I don't understand, I thought vaccines were safe." said Wesley's mom. "Also, what is the difference between injecting something into the body with a needle and ingesting toxins, such as mercury, from fish?"

Doctor Sandra explained that when we ingest mercury from food and water sources, our body filters out most of the toxins through our liver and kidneys; when we inject our body, it doesn't have a good chance of filtering it out of our systems. So, our immune system is being attacked and we will run fevers to defend our body. Many children have temporary reactions, but some are lifelong."

"I've had patients stop responding to their names and interacting with others."

"For the most part, the damage that is done to our bodies is extremely hard to reverse. Unfortunately, because the toxins go into the organs, such as the brain, they can cause major damage."

"You are one of the lucky ones, Wesley, I'm certain you'll make a full recovery."

She then looked at Wesley's mom and continued. "I always tell my patients it's up to them what they choose to do; it's their body so it should be their choice. But make sure to read the vaccine inserts found inside the vaccine boxes before you agree to anything, and make sure you have a good understanding of the ingredients listed and the reactions they can cause. Make sure you ask questions first."

Doctor Sandra reached into her desk drawer, pulled out a sheet of paper and handed it to Wesley's mom. "This gives directions for a detox to be done after vaccinations to help rid the body of toxins before they do more damage. There are suggestions for a gut detox, taking Omega 3 fatty acids, detox baths, and so much more. Also, this sheet has the contact information for a non-profit organization that educates people about the harm vaccines can cause."

"There is also a facts sheet with a list of vaccine ingredients that you may want to do some research on. Doing things more naturally will have a better impact on your health. She looked at Wesley and said a little more loudly so he would pay attention. "You build a healthy immune system by eating lots of fresh fruits and veggies and taking the vitamins your mom gives you—right Wesley?"

He grinned and nodded.

Doctor Sandra continued talking to Wesley's mom. "I must warn you though, you will face backlash from schools, doctors and the public. The fear is real and what people can't understand, they reject."

"Thank you so much, Doctor Sandra. This has really opened my eyes. From now on we won't be continuing with vaccinations. I am going to go home and dig deep into this."

"Go home and rest Wesley, put an ice pack where it is swollen and run a salt bath first thing when you get home. If anything changes, come back to see me," Doctor Sandra explained with a smile.

Wesley and his mom stood up to walk out and Doctor Sandra added, "Also, don't give him any pain relievers ever. They suppress the immune system, just like vaccines."

"I'll look into that too," said Wesley's mom. "Thanks again."

On the way to the car, Wesley's mom told him, "Things are going to be different now, Wesley. I'm going to do all I can to protect you and make sure this doesn't happen again. It's a new journey for both of us." She hugged her boy before buckling him up into his seat.

"Thanks, Mom," he said. "I AM one of the lucky ones."

Ingredients to Research

❏ Aluminum Toxicity

❏ Animal Products in Vaccines

❏ Fetal Cell Lines in Vaccines

❏ Vaccine Contaminants

❏ Aluminum Salts

❏ Lactose

❏ Polysorbate

❏ Gelatin

❏ Sucrose

❏ Fetal Bovine Serum

❏ Sodium Chloride

Written by Robyn Stevens

www.ingramcontent.com/pod-product-compliance
Lightning Source LLC
Chambersburg PA
CBHW042115040426
42448CB00003B/282